VENEZUELA

A TRUE BOOK

by

Ann Heinrichs

Children's Press®

A Division of Grolier Publishing

New York London Hong Kong Sydney
Danbury, Connecticut

Reading Consultant
Linda Cornwell
Learning Resource Consultant
Indiana Department of
Education

A Venezuelan Indian

Library of Congress Cataloging-in-Publication Data

Heinrichs, Ann.
   Venezuela / by Ann Heinrichs.
   p.   cm. — (A true book)
   Includes bibliographical references and index.
   Summary: A basic overview of the history, geography, climate, and
culture of Venezuela.
   ISBN 0-516-20344-4 (lib.bdg.)   0-516-26180-0 (pbk.)
   1. Venezuela—Juvenile literature. [1. Venezuela.] I. Title. II.
Series.
F2308.5.H45 1997
987—dc20   96-31629
                                            CIP
                                            AC

Contents

Mountains, Forests, and Plains

Venezuela is a country on the northern coast of South America. It lies along the Caribbean Sea, with the Atlantic Ocean on the northeast. Tall mountains line the seacoast. Venezuela's western neighbor is Colombia. To the south is Brazil, and on the east is Guyana.

The Maracaibo Basin surrounds Lake Maracaibo in western Venezuela. Lake Maracaibo is South America's largest lake.

The Andean Highlands stretch across northern Venezuela. Snow-capped Pico Bolívar, Venezuela's highest peak, rises in these mountains. Many farms and small towns nestle in the cool hills and valleys of the highlands.

At 16,000 feet (5,000 meters), Pico Bolívar (above) is the highest mountain in Venezuela. Many Venezuelans live and work on the waters of Lake Maracaibo (left).

The flat, grassy plains of Venezuela are called llanos.

The region called the llanos is a hot, dry grassy plain in central Venezuela. *Llaneros*, or cowboys, tend herds of cattle on the ranches of the llanos.

South of the llanos, the Orinoco River cuts across

Venezuela from west to east.
At the swampy Orinoco Delta in
the east, the Orinoco branches
into about fifty smaller streams.
Crocodiles slink among the
delta's mangrove trees.

The Orinoco River (left) is a
major waterway in Venezuela.
Crocodiles (right) are a common
sight along the Orinoco River.

South of the Orinoco, the Guyana Highlands cover half of Venezuela. Long ago, water and winds formed the area's flat-topped mountains and steep cliffs. Angel Falls tumbles down one of these cliffs. It is the highest water-fall in the world.

The far south and west are lush with rain forests and jungles. Toucans, macaws, and monkeys screech overhead.

Angel Falls is 3,212 feet (979 m) high—
the highest waterfall in the world.

People of Many Cultures

More than 21 million people live in Venezuela. Most of the population live along the northern coast of the country. About two of every three Venezuelans are descended from a mixture of Spanish, Indian, or African ancestors.

Most Venezuelans have a heritage that includes Spaniards, Indians, and Africans.

Venezuela's blacks are descended from slaves. Some slaves were brought from Africa. Other slaves came from Spanish colonies in the Caribbean region.

Most of Venezuela's Indians mixed with other races. Some Indians of unmixed ancestry still live in the rain forests and the Orinoco Delta. They hunt and fish as their ancestors did for thousands of years. The Yanomami are the largest Indian group.

Today, the descendants of Africans who were brought to Venezuela as slaves still live there (left). Some of Venezuela's Indians live in the rain forest as their ancestors did (right).

About nine of every ten Venezuelans live in cities or towns. Caracas, on the northern coast, is the capital and largest city. Very few people live south of the Orinoco River.

Caracas, Venezuela's capital, is home to more than one million people.

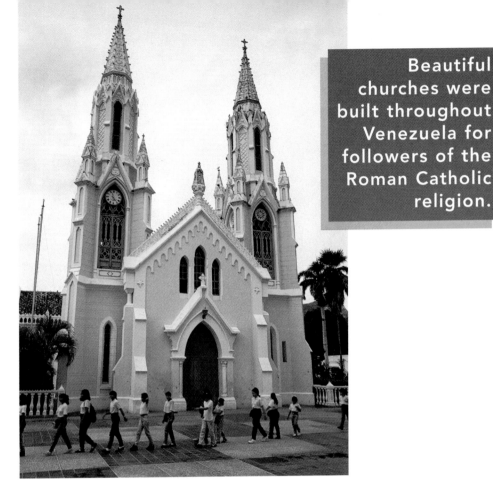

Most Venezuelans follow the Roman Catholic faith. African slaves also brought in their ancient folk beliefs, and Indians honor spirits found in the natural world around them.

Colonial Times

Early Spanish explorers in Venezuela saw huts along the edge of Lake Maracaibo. Indians traveled to their huts by canoe. This reminded the Spaniards of Venice, a city in Italy. Venice's streets are water canals, where people travel by boat. The Spaniards

Venezuela was named after Venice, Italy, where city streets are really canals.

named the country Venezuela, which means "Little Venice."

Indians lived in Venezuela long before the Spaniards arrived. The Arawak in the Andes region were farmers.

People living in the Andes Mountains use many of the farming methods that the Arawak Indians used.

They cut flat strips of farmland into hillsides. Called terraces, these hillside farms looked like stair steps. Carib indians lived in the eastern coastal regions.

Christopher Columbus was the first European to reach Venezuela. In 1498, he landed on the Paria Peninsula. The people who lived there wore ornaments of gold and pearls.

Christopher Columbus sailed to the Paria Peninsula of Venezuela in 1498.

San Antonio castle was constructed in Cumaná to defend the city from pirates.

Soon, Venezuela became a colony of Spain. In 1523, Spanish colonists founded the town of Cumaná, on the north coast. Today it is the oldest Spanish settlement in South America.

The colonists raised sugar-cane, tobacco, and cacao on their plantations. They also brought cattle to graze on the llanos. The colonists used Indians as slaves on the plantations.

Many plantations have been restored as museums and historic sites where visitors can learn more about Venezuela's history.

BIRTH OF A NATION

In 1811, Venezuelans were the first South Americans to demand independence from Spain. Ten years of fighting followed. Finally, led by Simón Bolívar, Venezuelans won their independence in 1821.

Venezuela joined with Colombia, Ecuador, and Panama to form the republic of Gran Colombia. In 1830, Venezuela became a separate country.

How People Live

Caracas, the capital of Venezuela, was founded in 1567. Since then, it has grown into a modern city. Throughout Caracas, old Spanish-style churches and homes still stand among high-rise buildings, shopping centers, and outdoor cafés.

In Caracas, old Spanish-style buildings stand next to modern buildings and stores.

To escape traffic jams, many people ride the high-speed subway train.

Barrios (top left) are overcrowded, dirty areas where many of Venezuela's poor people live. Many Venezuelans live in houses or apartments near cities (top right). Farmers usually live in smaller, one- or two-room houses (bottom).

Poor people live in crowded areas called barrios on the edges of towns. Their homes are shacks made of cardboard or metal, called ranchos. Many of these ranchos have no electricity or running water. The Venezuelan government is trying to improve life in the barrios by building public housing.

Middle-class people live in Spanish-style houses or large apartment buildings. Farmers in small villages live in simple homes with one or two rooms.

Venezuelans enjoy eating beef, chicken, and fish. The national bread is a cornmeal cake called *arepa*. *Pabellón crióllo*, a typical meal, is made of thin beef strips, black beans, and rice. Slices of plantain, a fruit that looks like a banana, are served with it.

Venezuelans are avid baseball fans. Every big city has its own major-league team. The champions go on to play in the Caribbean Series, a South

Outdoor markets sell
many of the foods that
Venezuelans enjoy.

Some Venezuelan towns have their own rodeos each year.

American version of the World Series. Soccer and basketball are popular, too. Many people also enjoy rodeos, horse racing, and bullfights.

Oil, Factories, and Farms

Venezuela is one of the world's leading oil-producing nations. Towering rigs in the Maracaibo Basin pump oil. This region holds the biggest supply of oil in South America. The eastern llanos are also rich in oil. Besides oil, Venezuela is rich in coal,

Oil rigs in the Maracaibo Basin (top); a Venezuelan mine (left)

iron, bauxite, diamonds, and gold.

Factories in Venezuela make steel, aluminum, paper, cloth, and machines. They also turn oil into chemicals and fuels. Most of the nation's factories are located along the northern coast of Venezuela.

Factories in Venezuela produce aluminum, cloth, machines, and other goods.

Cacao, the main ingredient in chocolate, grows on trees in Venezuela.

Coffee, cacao, rice, sugar-cane, corn, and bananas are important crops. They grow in the fertile soil of Venezuela's hillsides and valleys. Cattle ranches produce beef and milk.

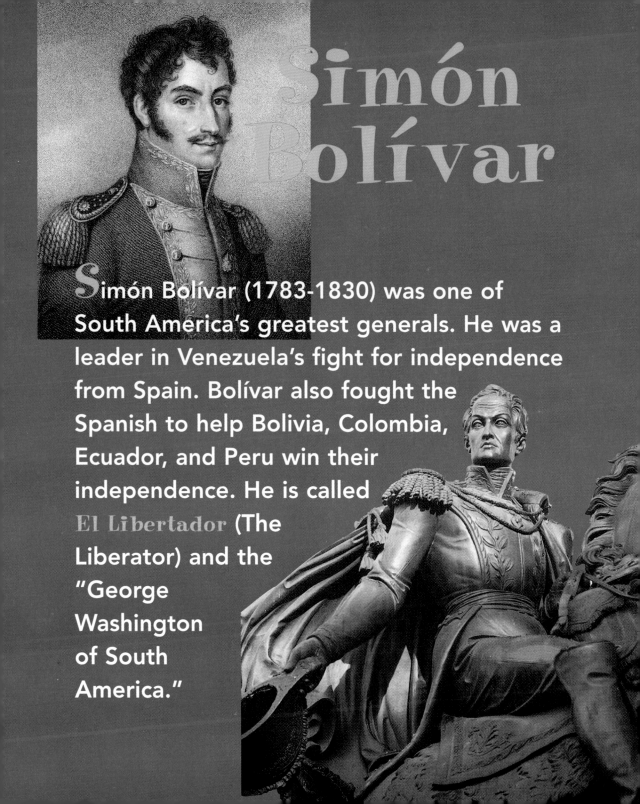

Simón Bolívar

Simón Bolívar (1783-1830) was one of South America's greatest generals. He was a leader in Venezuela's fight for independence from Spain. Bolívar also fought the Spanish to help Bolivia, Colombia, Ecuador, and Peru win their independence. He is called El Libertador (The Liberator) and the "George Washington of South America."

Festivals and Culture

Most Venezuelans enjoy festivals. They celebrate the feast days of Christian saints. Each region or town has its favorite festivals, which consist of music, dances, and parades.

The best-known festival in Venezuela is Carnaval. Each year, this springtime festival is

Venezuelans of all ages enjoy the costumes and makeup worn to celebrate Carnaval.

African culture can be found in many traditional dances, music, and customs of Venezuela.

held just before the Christian holy season of Lent. People fill the streets for days of fun with parades, dancing, and games.

African culture is also part of Venezuelan life. It appears in music, dance, folk tales, and religious customs. On the feast of Corpus Christi, blacks near Caracas perform a dance wearing traditional African masks.

The lively *joropo* is Venezuela's national folk dance. The men wear loose

Music is an important part of Venezuelan culture.

shirts and sashes, while the women wear colorful skirts and white blouses. Musicians shake rattles called maracas and play *cuatros* (four-stringed guitars). The merengue and the *guaracha* are Caribbean folk dances.

Venezuelans are proud of their country's long history. Together with their leaders, they will continue to make a good life, and a hopeful future, for all Venezuelans.

Venezuelans are working to create a bright future for the nation's children.

To Find Out More

Here are some additional resources to help you learn more about the nation of Venezuela:

 **Books**

 **Organizations**

Adler, David. **A Picture Book of Simón Bolívar.** Holiday House, 1992.

Fox, Geoffrey. **The Land and People of Venezuela.** HarperCollins, 1991.

Lerner Geography Department. **Venezuela in Pictures.** Lerner, 1993.

Lewington, Anna. **What Do We Know About: The Amazonian Indians?** Peter Bedrick Books, 1993.

United Nations Information Centre
1775 K Street, NW
Washington, D.C. 20008

Venezuelan Embassy
1099 30th Street, NW
Washington, D.C. 20007

Venezuelan American Association of the United States
150 Nassau Street, Room 2015
New York, NY 10038

Online Sites

Strange Birds
*http://swissnet.ai.mit.edu/
zoo/birds.html*

Great color photos of toucans and many other exotic birds

Venezuelan Amazon Expedition
*http://sunsite.doc.ic.ac.uk/
netspedition/amazon.html*

An exciting journey through Venezuela's Amazon forest, including maps, photos, geography, and wildlife

Venezuela for Kids
*http://venezuela.mit.edu/
embassy/kids/index.html*

All kinds of information on the country's history, political system, capital, folklore, sports, holidays, and more

Venezuela's Web Server
http://venezuela.mit.edu/

An interactive map of Venezuela, weather forecasts for Caracas, travel information, history, photos, language, food, links to personal home pages, and much more

Important Words

ancestors relatives who lived long ago

cacao seeds that are used to make cocoa, chocolate, or other products

colony territory owned or claimed by another country

culture the customs and beliefs of a group of people

highland land that is covered by mountains or hills

mangrove tropical tree with long roots that grows above the ground

plantation large estate or farm

public housing apartments built by the government for poor people

Index

Meet the Author

Ann Heinrichs grew up in Arkansas and lives in Chicago, Illinois. She has written more than twenty books about American, Asian, and African history and culture. She has also written numerous newspaper, magazine, and encyclopedia articles.

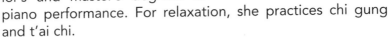

Besides the United States, she has traveled in Europe, North Africa, the Middle East, and east Asia. The desert is her favorite terrain.

Ms. Heinrichs holds bachelor's and master's degrees in piano performance. For relaxation, she practices chi gung and t'ai chi.

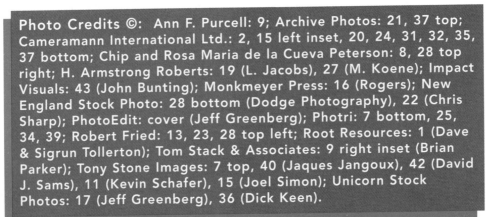